better together*

*This book is best read together, grownup and kid.

 akidsco.com

a
kids
book
about

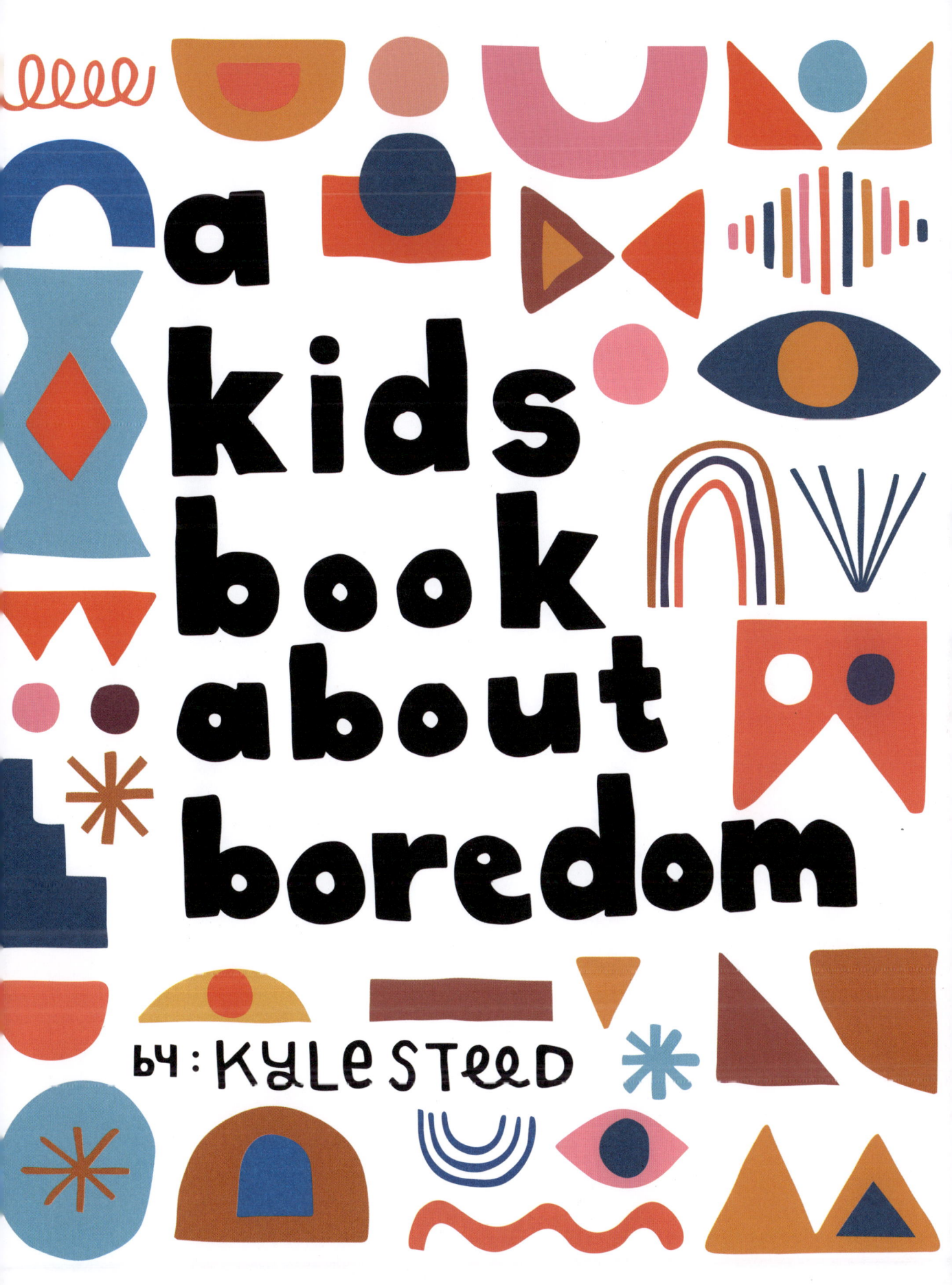

a kids book about boredom

by: KYLE STEED

A Kids Co.
Editor Denise Morales Soto
Designer Duke Stebbins
Illustrator Kyle Steed
Creative Director Rick DeLucco
Studio Manager Kenya Feldes
Sales Director Melanie Wilkins
Head of Books Jennifer Goldstein
CEO and Founder Jelani Memory

DK
Senior Production Editor Jennifer Murray
Senior Production Controller Louise Minihane
Senior Acquisitions Editor Katy Flint
Acquisitions Project Editor Sara Forster
Managing Art Editor Vicky Short
Managing Director, Licensing Mark Searle

First American edition, 2025
Published in the United States by DK Publishing, 1745 Broadway, 20th Floor,
New York, NY 10019

First published in Great Britain in 2025 by
Dorling Kindersley Limited, 20 Vauxhall Bridge Road, London SW1V 2SA
A Penguin Random House Company

The authorised representative in the EEA is
Dorling Kindersley Verlag GmbH. Arnulfstr. 124, 80636 Munich, Germany

A catalog record for this book is available from the Library of Congress.
A CIP catalogue record for this book is available from the British Library.
ISBN: 978-0-2417-4321-8

DK books are available at special discounts when purchased in bulk for sales
promotions, premiums, fund-raising, or education use. For details, contact:
DK Publishing Special Markets, 1745 Broadway, 20th Floor, New York, NY 10019
SpecialSales@dk.com

Printed and bound in China
www.dk.com
akidsco.com

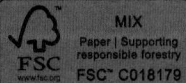

To my wife, Amanda, for meeting me where I'm at.

To both my girls, Savy and Geny,
who teach me the art of doing nothing.

And to every person I've met along the way—
each and every one of you is a gift.

Intro
for grownups

I'm bored already and haven't even written anything. Do you ever feel this way too? What do you do with that feeling of boredom? Do you look for ways to feel better and distract yourself?

I know, I get it, I do it sometimes too. But what are we doing when we prioritize our distractions instead of leaning into the void?

The space boredom makes for us is an amazing chance to be creative. To dream. To draw. To dance. There are no rules to being bored. There is you, me, and our imaginations. Go ahead, I dare you to be bored more.

Have you ever felt bored?

Have you ever felt like there's just nothing to do?

Or like you're missing out on something?

Have you ever felt like you should be doing something? Anything?

But you don't know what that something is?

Are you bored right now reading this book?

Well guess what...

Everyone gets bored.

But being bored can be a really good thing.

A wonderful thing, actually.

I know that may sound a little weird,
but just stay with me for a second.

I promise, it'll all make sense.

My name is *KYLE STEED*
and I get bored just like you.

When I was a kid, I was bored all the time, but I didn't know that being bored could be a good thing.

So a lot of the time, I felt really bad or guilty about being bored and not knowing what to do.

It took me a long time to learn to embrace boredom, but when I finally did, I realized that it was kind of like a *SUPERPOWER.*

My story as an artist *emerges* from being bored.

I paint and make images of all sizes and shapes. From large murals on the sides of buildings, to small works on canvas in my studio.

As an artist, I get bored SO easily!

But I rely on being bored to create.

what?! you may be thinking.

But it's true!

Because
when I'm bored,
I don't set out to draw a specific thing.

I just create for the sake of creating.

I figure it out as I go.

I don't think about making
something that's perfect
or even good.

I put pencil to paper
and see what comes out...

I figured out that most of the time, this happens when I have nothing to do and don't force myself to do something.

To tell you the truth...

being bored makes me a better artist.

I KNOW that can be hard to believe, because when you're bored it feels like it's impossible to do anything at all.

Well, I'm here to tell you that you actually don't have to do anything at all.

Doing nothing can be the most beautiful

and **powerful** thing in life.

So ~~JUST~~ BE Bored!

Make time to be bored.

Make a sign for your door that says:

(And see what happens!)

Lie down on the floor with your eyes closed and just think, or feel, or do nothing at all.

Or watch the clouds and see what shapes they make while you listen to the birds.

Or pay attention to how the wind feels against your skin and hair— and nothing else.

Sounds boring, right? Good.

Being bored is your **you** time.

Your time to explore what you think, what you feel, and what you love. Whatever that may be!

Let your IMAGINATION guide you.

Let your mind wander.

you
could...

make up a noise and imagine what it would sound like if it were yelled by your toaster, then dress up in clothes that don't fit you and pretend you're starting your own civilization in your lunch box, but the yogurt has gotten kinda smelly.

(You've got this!)

you could...

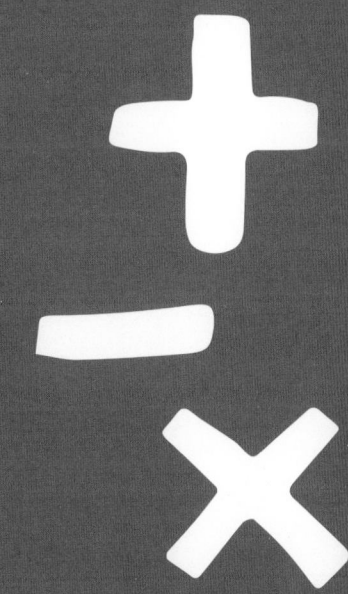

create a song on the spot about a silly
way to remember your math facts.

you CoULd...

take all your sheets, blankets, and pillows off your bed and stack them like warm pancakes in the middle of your room and pretend you're a giant having breakfast. (Yum!)

you could.

go out and look for bugs and
document their entire family tree
and where they came from.

you
could...

draw a picture of something that's not anything (but not with a pencil and definitely not on a piece of paper).

you
could...

start a podcast about the things you find hiding in the back of your closet.

LITERALLY anything.*

*Or nothing!

Not
everything
you do or

make needs to have a purpose.

Get in touch with yourself and do what comes naturally. Don't overthink it.

Making mistakes is part of the journey.

Trust yourself and know that it's OK
if you don't make the right
choice right away.

No one has to see it—unless you
want to show it to them.

This is for you first.

What happens after that is up to you.

So please, go ahead,
be bored and make mistakes.

you're welcome.*

*To be bored. Any time.

Outro
for grownups

OK, hopefully this book wasn't "boring" and instead has inspired a desire to cultivate more time to be bored. Over the coming days, weeks, or months, I hope you can carve out time in your schedule, and your kid's schedule, to do nothing. To sit. To play. To imagine. Mostly, to know that you're OK when you're not being productive. I've learned that by leaning into those feelings that kick and scream against the nothingness, I'm able to unearth a fear of the unknown. And once I accept the fear it almost instantly turns to vapor and my mind is clear again.

Some helpful tips to ease into this practice: Use the tools you have on hand. I like to set a timer for 20–30 minutes on my phone, turn on "Do Not Disturb" mode, and allow myself to use that time however I want. It can be sitting outside, taking in the trees and birds in my backyard. It can also look like pulling out some paper and pencils and letting my mind wander through images. No destination in mind. Enjoying the journey.

Made to empower.

a kids book about **racism**
by Jelani Memory

a kids book about ANXIETY
by Ross Szabo

a kids book about DISABILITY
by Kristine Napper

a kids book about IMAGINATION
by LEVAR BURTON

a kids book about belonging
by Kevin Carroll

a kids book about failure
by Dr Laymon Hicks

a kids book about GRATITUDE
by Ben Kenyon

a kids book about LIFE ONLINE
by Dave S. Anderson & Blake Fleischacker

a kids book about body image
by Rebecca Alexander

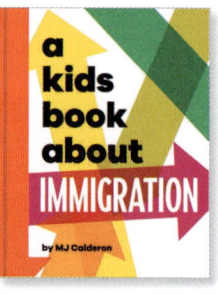
a kids book about IMMIGRATION
by MJ Calderon

a kids book about EMPATHY
by Daron K. Roberts

a kids book about GENDER
by Dale Mueller

a kids book about Love
by ZIGGY MARLEY

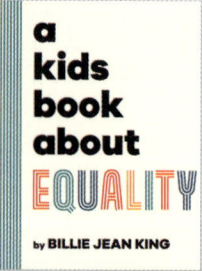
a kids book about EQUALITY
by BILLIE JEAN KING

a kids book about MONEY
by Adam Stramwasser

a kids book about FEMINISM
by Emma McIlroy

a kids book about adventure
by Dr Ben Tertin

a kids book about CLIMATE CHANGE
by Zanagee Artis & Olivia Greenspan

a kids book about CONFIDENCE
by Joy Cho

a kids book about BEING NONBINARY
by Hunter Chinn-Raicht

Discover more at akidsco.com